Original title:
Celestial Silliness

Copyright © 2025 Creative Arts Management OÜ
All rights reserved.

Author: Tobias Winslow
ISBN HARDBACK: 978-1-80567-832-8
ISBN PAPERBACK: 978-1-80567-953-0

Jupiter's Jocular Jester

On Jupiter's moons, they dance and prance,
With giggly glee in a jovial trance.
The clouds are laughing, swirling like cream,
While storms crack jokes in a thunderous meme.

The moons play chess with oversized pawns,
While Saturn's rings twirl in silly yawns.
A giant shrimp plays the accordion loud,
As the jovial jester bows to the crowd.

The Silly Symphony of Space

Planets march in a wobbly line,
Dancing to a tune that's simply divine.
Asteroids tap dance with comets in tow,
Creating a wacky, interstellar show.

Stars wear hats, to be extra absurd,
While Pluto bursts forth with a cheerful word.
The Milky Way sings a song of delight,
As black holes giggle and twinkle at night.

Rascally meteors

From the depths of dark, they zoom and glide,
With tails of laughter, they swiftly slide.
Rascally meteors, they race and tease,
Playing hide and seek 'neath the cosmic trees.

They throw cosmic pies at the moon so bright,
Creating a spectacle of pure silly sight.
Twinkling stars cheer and burst into song,
As the meteors prance, mischief all along.

Cosmic Capers

In a carousel of laughter, worlds go round,
Giggling satellites make the silliest sound.
Galaxies swirl in a whimsical spin,
While aliens chuckle, inviting you in.

Distant light beams hilariously sway,
In cosmic capers, they frolic and play.
With a wink and a nod, the cosmos ignites,
In a joyful ruckus of interstellar lights.

Reflective Radiance

Stars wear their shades at midnight,
Planets spin in dizzy delight,
Comets breakdance through the dark,
While moonbeams throw a spark.

Galaxies giggle in twirls,
As space dust sprinkles and swirls,
Shooting stars race for a laugh,
In this cosmic photograph.

Spunky Supernova

A star decided to burst with glee,
Flashing colors just to see,
Nebulas twirl in vibrant jest,
In the universe's silly quest.

Planets tease with cheeky orbits,
Winking at asteroids like hobbits,
Bouncing light years, doing tricks,
Creating space's jolly mix.

Giddy Galaxy Gatherings

Galaxies gather for a grand feast,
With cosmic cupcakes and lights at least,
Black holes tell jokes, they suck you in,
While superclusters twirl with a spin.

Asteroids play tag, dodging grand stars,
Twirling around those ancient cars,
With laughter echoing through the night,
It's a party in the endless light.

Jovial Journeys in the Skies

Rockets giggle on their way,
Through stardust paths where comets play,
Jupiter's moon shares a pun,
As Saturn's rings have tons of fun.

Astronauts float in zany styles,
Wearing helmets full of smiles,
With every leap a silly dance,
In the universe's boundless expanse.

Enigmatic Eclipses

The moon wore shades at noon, oh bright,
While planets danced in silly flight.
Stars juggled comets in a show,
As clouds turned pink with laughter's glow.

Saturn spilled its rings like candy,
And Mars found jokes that were quite dandy.
Nibbling on light from dusk till dawn,
The universe chuckled, came and gone.

Galactic Giggles

A meteor flew past with a grin,
As asteroids twirled with reckless spin.
Nebulae painted in hues of glee,
Tickling astrological symmetry.

Venus wore a hat, quite absurd,
While Jupiter sang each silly word.
Galaxies tickled with gentle quirks,
In the great void, where hilarity lurks.

Chuckling in the Cosmos

In the depths where bright stars collide,
Whispers of laughter took a wild ride.
Quasars giggling across the night,
Winking at comets with pure delight.

Pulsars ticked in rhythm and rhyme,
Spreading light-hearted joy through time.
In every shadow, a prankster's face,
The cosmos chuckled in joyful grace.

Starry-Eyed Mischief

Twinkling eyes among the void,
In their merriment, they were overjoyed.
Little sprites danced on solar flares,
In playfulness, no one dared compare.

Black holes grinned, pulling stardust tight,
While supernovas burst with sheer delight.
Astral jesters cavorted, oh what a sight!
In the grand scheme, everything felt right.

Dancing Planets

In a swirl of colors bright,
Planets twirl, what a sight.
Mars does the tango with flair,
While Venus spins without a care.

Jupiter jumps with a loud boom,
Saturn giggles, shakes its plume.
Carefree moons join in the fun,
Under the gaze of a joking sun.

Cosmic Chuckles

Stars wink mischievously high,
As comets zoom and then fly by.
Nebulas puff with a giggly sigh,
While black holes grin, oh my, oh my!

Asteroids wobble, clash, then sway,
Silly sprites causing a fray.
Each twinkle tells a cheeky tale,
In this vastness, no room to pale.

Laughter Among the Stars

Constellations chat in bright robes,
Making jokes from their cosmic probes.
Orion tells tales of lost socks,
While Ursa continues to tick, it clocks.

The Milky Way chuckles at night,
Spreading giggles of pure delight.
Every star has a quip to bestow,
As they sparkle and shimmer, don't you know?

The Whimsical Orbit

A sly moon dances in the night,
Winking at Earth with all its might.
Planets play a merry round,
Echoing laughter all around.

Galaxies swirl in a grand ballet,
Creating joy that brightens the way.
Each orbit spins with comic grace,
In this lighthearted, starry space.

The Starstruck Comedy Club

In the cosmic hall of laughter bright,
Jupiter juggles, oh what a sight!
Mercury tries a stand-up act,
But trips on a comet, that's a fact!

Saturn spins jokes with rings so wide,
While Mars tosses giggles, full of pride.
The stars all chuckle, the moons all sway,
As laughter echoes through the Milky Way.

Sunbeams' Playful Pranks

Sunbeams sneak in with a glint in their rays,
Tickling the planets in mischievous ways.
Neptune wears shades, thinking he's cool,
While Venus plays tag, breaking all the rules!

The Earth spins dizzy, laughs turn to spins,
While clouds throw giggles like fluffy white sins.
Lightning bolts scribble on the night sky,
With punchlines so bright, everyone is awry.

Whimsies of the Wide Universe

Galaxies twirl in a whimsical dance,
Cosmic mice moonwalk, given the chance.
Galactic giggles fill black holes with cheer,
As asteroids laugh, we hear them quite clear!

Quasars waltz with a wink and a twirl,
While planets play hopscotch, oh what a whirl!
Supernovas burst forth with sparkling glee,
And comets come in for a zany spree.

Space-Bound Shenanigans

Rockets zoom past with a honk and a beep,
While aliens dance in a flicker of sheep.
Gravity giggles as they float around,
A dance party starts on the glowing ground!

Stars wear bowties for a jolly big show,
While moons do the cha-cha, stealing the glow.
Asteroids tumble, all in good fun,
As laughter erupts, turning night into sun.

Silly Satellites

In orbit they dance, with glee and delight,
Spinning in circles, oh what a sight!
They giggle and twirl, they pull silly faces,
As Earth looks up, it chuckles in places.

One jumps out of line, gives a stuck-out tongue,
While another spins faster, just for some fun!
They throw moonbeams like frisbees at night,
As the stars laugh along, what a playful sight!

Cosmic Pranks

The comets come racing, with tails full of tricks,
Leaving behind them a shower of flicks.
They tickle the planets, they tease the sun's rays,
Turning serious worlds into giggling displays.

Venus wears glasses, so funny and bright,
Jupiter jumps in, oh what a delight!
They sneak up on Saturn, tickle its rings,
And watch as it wobbles and dances and sings!

Mischievous Meteorites

Shooting through night with a glimmering dash,
They wink and they giggle, they fly full of sass.
With a whirling flurry, they make quite a scene,
While Earth holds its breath, caught between beams.

Hitting the atmosphere with a playful *pop*,
They burst into laughter, their antics won't stop.
Plans to hide under clouds, oh what a disguise,
As they tumble around like sweet little spies!

Astral Absurdities

Up in the sky, where nonsense is key,
Stars dress in costumes—what silliness, we see!
A star in a tutu, and one with a hat,
Giggles erupt as the moon joins their chat.

They play cosmic chess with the black holes for fun,
Each move gets a laugh, and a spark of the sun.
In galaxies bright, the laughter takes flight,
With absurdities swirling throughout the night!

Stellar Sillies

Stars wear hats made of cheese,
Planets bounce in cosmic breeze.
Jupiter jingles, Saturn sings,
Galaxies dance on fluffy wings.

Comets zoom with playful flair,
While asteroids play hide and share.
The moon tells jokes to passing meteors,
Laughter echoes through time's corridors.

In this vast and joyous space,
Silly shadows intermingle with grace.
Each twinkle giggles with a wink,
While starlight dips into a drink.

So join the fun, don't be shy,
Laugh with the stars, give it a try!
For in the night, with jesters bright,
Cosmic chuckles fill the sky.

Solar Smirks

The sun wears shades and strikes a pose,
Tickling planets from head to toes.
Mercury spins, full of delight,
While Venus giggles, shining bright.

Mars tells tales of Martian pranks,
While Saturn winks, with playful flanks.
Neptune whispers with a chuckling glow,
Sending smiles to those below.

The solar winds are full of cheer,
Blowing laughter for all to hear.
Eclipses play hide and seek,
In a game of giggles, never bleak.

So bask in rays of warmth and glee,
Dance with the sun, come join the spree!
With every dawn, a joker's show,
Reflecting light in a joyful glow.

Lightearted Lunations

The moon pulls pranks on tides and seas,
Winking at clouds with utmost ease.
Full faces glow with mischief sweet,
As dreams soar high on silver feet.

Stars gather round for moonlit fun,
Whispering secrets till the night is done.
A twinkling laugh in the cosmos' play,
Makes night feel bright, come what may.

Lanterns of light dance on the breeze,
While comets giggle, swaying trees.
In the grandeur of night's embrace,
Silliness shines in every space.

So tip your hat to the moon's delight,
Join the laughter, feel the light!
For under the stars, life's a jest,
A whimsical ride, let's be our best.

Euphoria of the Expanse

In the void, where laughter sings,
Quasars flutter with sparkly wings.
Spirals twist, parade in style,
While photons grin and beams beguile.

Kites of stardust soar on high,
Catch the giggles floating by.
Each nebula a canvas bright,
Painted with joy, a glorious sight.

Gravity trips on unseen thread,
As orbiting clowns go merrily ahead.
Laughter spirals like a cosmic tune,
Tickling the vastness, from sun to moon.

So leap through the stars, don't delay,
Join the cosmic circus, dance and play!
In the euphoria of the expanse,
Let silly souls enjoy the dance.

Lunatic Lunars

In a dance of cheese and mirth,
The moon made friends with the earth.
They giggled, spun, and twirled in glee,
Creating shadows for all to see.

Craters filled with laughter bright,
As lunar rabbits took to flight.
They bounced across the silver sea,
With sassy hops, so wild and free.

Stars donned hats of pink and blue,
Sipping tea from clouds anew.
Each sip a splash of shining fun,
A party raged 'til rise of sun.

With cosmic jokes they shared all night,
Their chuckles echoed, pure delight.
The universe caught in a spin,
Where silliness could surely begin.

Spirited Shooting Stars

Shooting stars on wobbly trails,
Whisper secrets, spin their tales.
They race and tumble through the sky,
While giggling at the clouds nearby.

A comet wearing rainbow shades,
Chased by meteors in parades.
With every flash, they laugh and cheer,
As the cosmos joins the fun, sincere.

Each flash ignites a spark of glee,
A cosmic dance for all to see.
They trip and fall with joyful grace,
In starry realms, a frolicsome race.

With candy trails and sprinkles bright,
They paint the heavens, pure delight.
Galactic giggles fill the night air,
As shooting stars declare, beware!

Mirthful Moons

The moon donned shades and danced around,
With a waltz of whimsy, not a sound.
Her craters filled with bouncing glee,
As funny faces shouted, "Whee!"

Lunar pirates in a jolly crew,
Set sail on beams of silver hue.
With giggles echoing through the night,
They tossed about their treasure bright.

A slinky moonbeam caught a breeze,
Entwined with dreams and flying keys.
They juggled stars, a cosmic clown,
While comets wore the silliest crown.

In moonlit capers, laughter soared,
With every chuckle, joy restored.
The galaxy twinkled, gleeful mirth,
As moons imbibed the joy of Earth.

Witty Wavelengths

In a world where waves can chat,
They giggle, wiggle, splish, and splat.
The ocean laughed with cosmic cheer,
As wavelengths danced without a fear.

Sound waves wore mismatched socks,
Tickling echoes, hopping rocks.
From whispers soft to shouts so loud,
They formed a silly, noisy crowd.

Vibrations played a prank and swayed,
As silly signals cavorted, played.
With boisterous beats and rhythmic prance,
They spun the cosmos in a dance.

In this jumbled, joyful space,
Every frequency found its place.
Chasing giggles through the air,
Witty wavelengths, free and rare.

Galactic Guffaws

Stars wore hats, quite so absurd,
Planets danced with laughter, stirred.
Jupiter jumped in playful glee,
While space cats purred with zero gravity.

Comets laughed as they flew by,
Whispering jokes that made us cry.
Asteroids tumbled in a twirl,
While moons giggled, doing a whirl.

Nebulas painted smiles so bright,
Sprinkling joy in the deep, dark night.
Quasars chuckled, their light a gleam,
In the vastness, we shared a dream.

Black holes yawn with a silly grin,
Swallowing laughter we dare to spin.
In this cosmos, funny and free,
We find the jest in infinity.

The Humor of Halos

Angels wear socks that don't quite match,
Heavenly giggles, an everyday catch.
Choirs sing off-key for a laugh,
As halos spin in a whimsical draft.

Clouds take selfies, capturing fun,
While rainbows chase after the sun.
Seraphs tumble in laughter, peals,
In a sky where humor reveals.

St. Bernard's angels lose their way,
Barking jokes as they frolic and play.
Cherubs hiding behind the stars,
Snickering softly in spaces afar.

All while galaxies twirl in delight,
Creating mischief in the silent night.
In the heavens where silliness reigns,
We find humor in joy's refrains.

Comedic Constellations

Orion dropped his sword with a clank,
While Puppis wagged its fluffy flank.
Ursa Major sang a silly tune,
As stars twinkled faintly like marooned balloons.

Andromeda stumbled, lost in the strewn,
Chasing her tail in a cosmic cartoon.
Draco laughed, drawing giggles from afar,
Spinning jokes like a bright shooting star.

Cassiopeia posed, ever so grand,
While Pegasus performed with a commanding hand.
The sky was alive with a joyous spark,
Creating a jest that lit up the dark.

Planets joined in with a comical cheer,
Laughter echoed throughout every sphere.
In this vast expanse, oh what delight,
As the universe laughs through the night.

Moonlight Mirth

The moon wore glasses, quite out of place,
Shining bright with a cheerful face.
Crickets chirped in perfect chime,
As shadows danced in a silly rhyme.

Silver beams tickled the earth's skin,
While stars entered a whimsical spin.
Night critters gathered for a show,
Under giggling skies in a magical glow.

Luna winked to the clouds above,
Sending down whispers of playful love.
Deep in the night, where mischief thrives,
We found our joy in the moonlit jives.

With giggles echoing through the trees,
The night wrapped us in a light breeze.
Moonlight laughter, a whimsical sight,
In the cradle of dark, we felt the light.

Whimsical Wonderment Above

In a cloud of cotton candy blue,
A giggling moon sings a tune or two.
Stars dance around with silly hats,
While comets race like playful cats.

Bubbles float in the sky so high,
Chasing dreams that refuse to fly.
Laughter echoes in the velvet night,
As starlight twinkles with pure delight.

Jupiter juggles its moons for fun,
While Saturn strums rays from the sun.
Nebulas swirl in hues of joy,
Making the cosmos a grand old toy.

Galaxies spin in a dizzy tale,
Where laughter floats on a wondrous gale.
Every spark in the dark brings cheer,
Oh, what a silly sight up here!

Raucous Ray of the Sun

The sun wore shades, a goofy grin,
Casting shadows with a silly spin.
Its rays bounced off the lake with glee,
Creating ripples of jubilee.

Birds in hats began to play,
Singing tunes to greet the day.
A breeze that giggled through the trees,
Brought chuckles carried on the breeze.

Sunflowers danced with flailing arms,
Waving proudly in their sunny charms.
Each petal flutters with such style,
Making even grumpy bugs smile.

As the day fades into night,
Fireflies spark in sheer delight.
Their tiny lanterns floating low,
Light up the world with their soft glow.

Hysterical Horizons

At dawn, a rooster starts to squeak,
It tells the world to take a peek.
Horizon stretches, yawning wide,
As giggles spill across the tide.

Mountains wear caps of fluffy white,
Pretending they're marshmallows in flight.
Twinkling streams chuckle as they flow,
Bubbles burst out in a joyful show.

Rainbows hop from cloud to cloud,
Daring the sun to join the crowd.
While butterflies wear shoes so bright,
Flapping around in sheer delight.

As night creeps in with a soft sigh,
Stars blurt out a twinkling pie,
They wink at the moon, light as a song,
In this silly world, we all belong.

Sparkling Stardust Shenanigans

In the realm where the stardust plays,
Cosmic critters parade in a haze.
They juggle planets, spin them quick,
With laughter that makes the meteors tick.

Galactic giants in bright bow ties,
Twist their mustaches under starry skies.
Asteroids tumble in a frolicsome race,
A raucous celebration in this vast space.

Hopping on asteroids with goofy cheers,
Aliens toast with fizzy spheres.
Nebulae swirl like cotton-wool fluff,
In this scene, there's never enough!

Shooting stars throw confetti wide,
While black holes open with fun inside.
Each little spark ignites the night,
In this whimsical dance of delight!

Silly Starwells

In a dance of twinkling lights,
Stars wear hats and dance at night.
They giggle as they twirl and spin,
Gravity's lost, let the fun begin.

Planets play leapfrog in the dark,
Comets leave trails like dogs in the park.
Moonbeams tickle, they shine and glow,
Chasing each other, putting on a show.

Galaxies swirl in a playful chase,
Whirling confetti in a starlit race.
Asteroids juggle, what a sight,
As Martians chuckle, laughing with delight.

Supernovae burst, like fireworks bright,
Shooting sparkles, oh what a sight!
In this vast theater, laughter takes flight,
As the universe giggles deep into the night.

Jovial Infinity

In the vastness of time, a hoot and a cheer,
Cosmic muffins are baked, it's party time here.
Saturn's rings spin like a carnival ride,
While Pluto throws confetti, feeling the pride.

Each quasar twinkles with a wink and a grin,
Wobbling through space like a toddler's spin.
They play hide and seek with the old black hole,
Where playfulness bubbles, and laughter's the goal.

Galactic giggles echo through space,
In nebula dance, stars find their pace.
With every twinkle, a pun is delivered,
As these cosmic clowns make the light shimmer.

So travel the skies, embrace the delight,
With whimsy and joy in the velvety night.
Infinity's funny, don't ever forget,
In this boundless playground, there's no regret!

Radiant Revelries

In a field of dreams where the comets play,
Shooting stars dress up in a bright cabaret.
Jupiter's juggling with a graceful twirl,
While Venus giggles, giving it a whirl.

Astro-bunnies bounce through the glowing fields,
Dancing on stardust, see how it yields.
Twirling like galaxies, all shapes and spins,
Catch the laughter before it begins.

Superheroes dress up as shooting stars,
Armored in laughter, dancing on Mars.
With every bounce, a new joke appears,
As laughter lights up all the cosmic spheres.

So join the revelry, put on your best cheer,
In the space of laughter, there's nothing to fear.
With radiant giggles that shine like the sun,
In this joyous expanse, let's all have some fun!

Ticklish Telescopes

Through lenses of wonder, we gaze at the night,
With telescopes chuckling, what a lovely sight!
They point and they tease, revealing the stars,
   Ticklish and tricky, just like candy bars.

A wink from a planet, a giggle on Mars,
As stardust dances in beams from afar.
Neptune whispers secrets, so silly and bright,
   Tickling the edges of the velvet night.

Our lofty devices, they wiggle and sway,
with cosmic quips that brighten the day.
Through lenses of laughter, they capture the glee,
   Inviting us all into their comedy spree.

So peer through the glass, let the joy be told,
In the realm of the stars, adventures unfold.
With every tickle, a universe grand,
In the funny embrace of the vast wonderland.

Whirling Whizz of the Milky Way

Stars are dancing, twirling bright,
Chasing comets in their flight.
Wobbling planets join the spree,
Giggling through infinity.

Nebulas puff like candy floss,
Planets find they cannot cross.
One bounces back, another breaks,
Laughing hard at cosmic pranks.

Galaxies spin in a playful race,
Tickling each other in open space.
Each twist and turn a joyous ride,
In the vastness where dreams collide.

Asteroids roll like playful jesters,
Juggling moons, what cosmic testers!
While shooting stars take turns to shine,
In this whirling lane, all's divine.

Capering Celestials

Bright meteor showers, a silly sight,
Shimmering trails, pure delight.
Venus giggles, Mars takes a spin,
As Saturn's rings play hide and seek within.

Moons wear hats, a funny fashion,
While stars explode with joyous passion.
Uranus sports a goofy pose,
As laughter in space continually flows.

Jupiter hops on a trampoline,
Bouncing high, as though it's keen.
The cosmos bursts with giddy cheer,
While starlight winks from far and near.

With a twirl and a swirl, the orbits play,
In the grand dance of the Milky Way.
In this merry realm, the fun ignites,
As cosmic capers fill endless nights.

Amusing Ascensions

Stars ascend like silly sprites,
Skimming clouds in bubble flights.
Planets giggle, wobble high,
As they bounce across the sky.

A comet wears a silly grin,
Spinning tales of where it's been.
Asteroids chuckle, take a leap,
In a cosmic dance that makes us weep.

Black holes yawn with a big surprise,
Swallowing light, then laughing cries.
Wormholes twist in a jester's bow,
Making paths we can't figure out how.

Constellations play tag on high,
Giving chase to the shooting by.
With each playful, starry rise,
The universe winks with joyful eyes.

Valiant Voyages through the Void

Spaceships zoom with quirks galore,
Spinning like tops, they might just soar.
Crew of aliens, hats askew,
Sailing through skies of vibrant hue.

Planets' antics, a wild race,
One slips on ice, yet keeps its grace.
Rocket fuel gives a hearty cheer,
As they blast off, never fear.

With giggles echoing through the dark,
They chase meteors, leave a spark.
Through the void, they march with flair,
In this grand quest they gladly share.

Each turn a chuckle, each dive a shout,
Finding laughter where there's no route.
On valiant voyages, they soar high,
Bringing joy to the cosmic sky.

Quirky Comets

Zooming through the starry night,
With wobbly tails and colorful light.
They dance and twirl, a silvery sight,
Making wishes feel just right.

One sneezed with a glittery blast,
Then tripped over the Moon quite fast.
They giggle and laugh, the moments amassed,
As they race through the heavens, unsurpassed.

A comet wearing a silly hat,
Cracks jokes with the planets, oh what a spat!
They tumble together, all chitchat,
In a cosmic ballet where dreams are at.

Watch them swirl, not caring at all,
As they giggle and spin, they are bound to fall.
With a wink and a smile, they heed the call,
Creating laughter in the vast cosmic hall.

Giggling Galaxies

In a whirl of laughter, stars take flight,
Spinning tales in the velvet night.
Galactic chuckles echo so bright,
While planets spin with pure delight.

Twinkling stars play peek-a-boo,
They sway and giggle, what a view!
Drawing in comets like a playful crew,
Creating a riot right out of the blue.

One galaxy dons a polka-dot gown,
While another spins and barrels down.
They share funny stories, never a frown,
In the vast universe, they wear the crown.

From spirals of joy, a dance does emerge,
As stardust spills in a harmonious surge.
With cosmic cheer, emotions urge,
To wrap the cosmos in a giggly purge.

Jovian Jests

On giant Jovian clouds, they float,
With laughter ringing in a cosmic coat.
Jokes crackle as stars begin to gloat,
While Saturn's rings keep them remote.

A jovial flare shot high and wide,
Tickling the moons that just can't hide.
They burst with laughter, opened wide,
As they skateboard down the planet's slide.

A mischievous wink from a bright red spot,
Leads to silliness that can't be caught.
With whirlwinds of fun, they spin the plot,
In the jovial sky, joy is never bought.

With comet friends making a wild fuss,
They drip with joy, not making a fuss.
In the realm of gas, they always trust,
Laughter and whimsy, a must.

Stellar Chuckles

Stars gather 'round for a galactic glee,
Cracking up beneath the cosmic sea.
Each twinkle a giggle, wild and free,
Tossing stardust in a cosmic spree.

A shooting star got tangled in wit,
Spinning with laughter, it couldn't sit.
With each burst of joy, they never admit,
That space is a stage for a hilarious skit.

Moonbeams peek in with a cheeky grin,
While the sun rolls its rays, taking a spin.
In this vibrant whirl, they all join in,
Whirling and twirling—let the fun begin!

As stars share secrets in endless flight,
Their chuckles echo through the velvet night.
With a sprinkle of humor, all feels right,
In the galaxy's heart, joy shines bright.

Saturn's Sassy Rings

Round and round the planet spins,
With rings that jiggle like silly twins.
Dancing dust in a cosmic dance,
Winking stars join in for a glance.

They twirl and swirl with sparkling flair,
Whispering secrets in the solar air.
Joking asteroids join for the ride,
In a giggly galaxy, they don't hide.

Rings are like hula hoops of fun,
Orbiting Saturn, they're never done.
Laughing comets race by so fast,
In this cosmic circus, joy is cast.

So if you look up on a clear night,
You might catch a glimpse of this silly sight.
With Saturn's rings and a wink or two,
The universe giggles just for you.

Nebulae Nonsense

In a cloud of color where stars are born,
They throw a party at the break of dawn.
Gassy giggles spill from the light,
As they dance around, oh what a sight!

With hiccuping hues and a whimsical glow,
They twist and twirl in a beautiful show.
Galactic clowns in a heavenly jest,
Making mischief, they never rest.

Whirling shapes with playful cheer,
Nebulae tease in a cosmic sphere.
A splash of purple, a wink of blue,
Painting the cosmos like a funny zoo.

So when you gaze at the night so wide,
Remember the laughter that they can't hide.
Each twinkling dot whispers funny lore,
In the vibrant tapestry of the galactic floor.

Asteroid Antics

Bouncing asteroids on a cosmic path,
Making silly faces that provoke a laugh.
Rolling round with a clunky cheer,
Creating chaos as they bounce near.

Whizzing through space with a hickory shamble,
Juggling moons, what a funny gamble!
"Oh, catch me if you can!" one cries,
While another tumbles with gleeful sighs.

They paint the void with whimsical flair,
Their rocky shapes dance free in air.
Playing tag in the silent abyss,
Asteroid antics, you wouldn't want to miss!

So imagine them racing in playful delight,
Chasing each other through the starry night.
In the cosmic playground, they freely prance,
Adding laughter to the universe's dance.

Twinkling Tickle Fights

Stars giggle softly, their lights all aglow,
Tickling the darkness with a gentle show.
Caught in a riddle of celestial glee,
Spreading sparkles like confetti spree.

In a battle of light, they shimmer and spark,
Poking and prodding in the cosmic dark.
"Oh, who's there?" one asks with a grin,
As stardust tickles the cheeky wind.

Comets zoom by with a whoosh and a twirl,
Joining the fun in a swirling whirl.
Twinkling stars laugh, sharing a wink,
Playing together in a cosmic pink.

So when night falls and you look above,
Remember the laughter, the light, and the love.
For in the sky, beneath the moon's light,
The stars are laughing in a ticklish fight.

Constellation Conundrums

Stars gather for a dance at night,
Twinkling with giggles, oh what a sight!
Scorpions tickle the moons up high,
While bears get lost in the starry sky.

A laugh escapes from Orion's belt,
As a comet trips, feels quite the melt.
The Leo lion leaps, but lands on a star,
And suddenly wonders, 'How did we get this far?'

The Big Dipper spills its liquid light,
While satellites fumble in their flight.
Galaxies wobble, giving a cheer,
For cosmic blunders, we hold so dear.

In the vastness, where fun meets grace,
Every twinkle wears a silly face.
So laugh along with the cosmic crew,
For the night sky loves a joke or two!

Bumbling Black Holes

In a corner of space, black holes collide,
Gravitational blunders they cannot hide.
They gobble up stars like a cosmic feast,
While forgetting their manners, to say the least.

With a great big yawn, they suck in the light,
Then wonder, 'Where'd it go? Was it really that bright?'
They trip over asteroids, rolling around,
Wishing they'd pay more attention to sound.

These voids sometimes giggle, it's odd but true,
They chuckle at planets just passing through.
With a whoosh and a swish, they're off to play,
In a game of hide and seek, night turns to day!

So if you spot one, give it a wink,
For black holes love to mess with your blink.
In their playful pull, we laugh without care,
For in their bumbling, there's joy everywhere!

Orbiting Oddities

Planets spin in a dizzying chase,
Twirling with giggles, they frolic in space.
A gas giant juggles clouds up high,
While a rocky friend attempts to fly.

Moons play tag, their course a dance,
As asteroids munch on cosmic chance.
In the rings of Saturn, a party unfolds,
With confetti of ice and dazzling golds.

Each comet that streaks brings laughter anew,
With tails of mischief that sweep right through.
Uranus spins sideways, what a delight!
It winks at Venus, who giggles outright.

So look to the heavens, where oddness frolics,
Stars and their friends are all comic chronicles.
For in the grand scheme of light-years and fun,
It's the quirks of the cosmos that keep us as one!

Gravity's Goofiness

Gravity plays tricks, a joker so sly,
Pulling us down while we leap to the sky.
With a hop and a skip, we float for a while,
Then land with a plop, and giggle and smile.

Bouncing on moons, we sway with delight,
Floating in dreams through the magical night.
Like space-bound clowns on a trampoline,
We soar and we tumble, so silly, so keen.

Down on the ground, we fumble and fall,
While meteors laugh at our stumble and sprawl.
In the dance of the cosmos, we find our own beat,
For gravity's mischief is pure comic treat.

So embrace the absurd in the vastness above,
For each merry mishap is sprinkled with love.
In the dance of the stars, we chuckle and play,
For life's silly moments make bright our day!

Wandering Whimsy

In a world where clouds wear hats,
And rainbows dance like acrobats,
The moon plays tag with stars on high,
While comets giggle as they fly.

A wise old owl recites a rhyme,
As squirrels juggle nuts, sublime,
The sun winks at the playful breeze,
Tickling flowers with such ease.

In fields of grass where laughter grows,
A whispering wind twirls with prose,
Each blade of green joins in the cheer,
As critters gather, smiles appear.

So chase the dreams that float on by,
With silly thoughts that reach the sky,
For in this land of jest and glee,
The heart can roam and wander free.

Daring Doodles in the Dark

In twilight's glow, the stars conspire,
To draw the whims of wild desire,
With crayons bright, the night is sketched,
While giggling ghosts play games, bewitched.

The moon slips on a cap and cloak,
As shadows tease with every joke,
A laughter echo fills the night,
As fireflies twinkle, pure delight.

With every stroke, a tale unfolds,
Of ticklish trolls and brave bears bold,
They dance on paper, upside down,
The night is ruled by whimsy's crown.

So grab your doodle, join the fun,
As night transforms till morning's sun,
For in this world of ink and spark,
Every laugh ignites the dark.

Jovial Jupiter Jive

Round and round the planet spins,
With jovial jigs and cheeky sins,
Galactic games on cosmic floors,
As planets giggle, roll, and soar.

Oh, how the moons play tag and chase,
Around the rings, they twist and race,
With every orbit comes a cheer,
As starry friends draw ever near.

Jupiter laughs with jovial glee,
While meteors dance, wild and free,
A symphony of silly sounds,
In every corner, joy abounds.

So float along this zany ride,
Where laughter through the cosmos glides,
Each twinkling light a wink and grin,
In this bright realm, let joy begin.

Hilarious Helios

Oh, Helios beams with a cheeky grin,
As sunspots waltz, let the fun begin,
He tickles clouds that float by high,
While shadows play the silliest spy.

With each ray, a giggle spins,
They frolic, skip, and twist their fins,
The sun's warm glow can't help but tease,
As nature laughs with playful ease.

Bright daisies bow with joy and flair,
Spinning in circles, pollens in the air,
Every petal shakes a silly groove,
In harmony, they find their move.

So bask in light and dance around,
Where laughter echoes, joy is found,
In the warmth of day, let spirits soar,
For hilarity calls, we crave for more.

Whimsical Wonders of the Sky

Up above, the stars do wink,
They giggle softly, don't you think?
Comets dance with joyful prance,
In the dark, they love to dance.

Clouds wear hats, so brightly spun,
Tickling the sun, oh what fun!
A moonbeam rides a silver kite,
Chasing shadows through the night.

Giggles echo from the breeze,
Whispers float among the trees.
The universe, a circus grand,
Full of laughs across the land.

Stars play tag in the velvet deep,
While sleepy planets drift and leap.
A meteoroid with a silly hat,
Winks and waves, just like that!

Playful Planets

Jupiter juggles, oh so wide,
While Saturn spins with rings of pride.
Mars wears red, a clownish hue,
While Venus winks, as if to cue.

Pluto grins, though far away,
Playing hide and seek all day.
Mercury zooms, a speedy chap,
Zipping through the cosmic map.

In a galaxy of giggly glee,
The stars all laugh, come see, come see!
Each little planet takes a turn,
To show off tricks, oh how we yearn!

With cosmic jokes and starry puns,
The sky is filled with silly runs.
A space parade of laughter bright,
Bringing joy in the deep, dark night.

Astrological Antics

Astrologers with goofy hats,
Draw charts of cats and silly bats.
They say the stars have tales to share,
Of goofy things that float in air.

Uranus grumbles, such a tease,
While Neptune giggles with the breeze.
The sun, a jester in their play,
Sprinkles laughter every day.

The zodiac signs, a motley crew,
Dance to tunes that feel brand new.
From Aries' prance to Pisces' splash,
They swap their jokes in cosmic flash.

A cosmic picnic on the moon,
Where laughter echoes, bright and strewn.
With asteroids playing leapfrog games,
The universe delights in names.

Nebula Nonsense

In a swirl of colors bright,
Nebulas giggle, what a sight!
With puffs of purple, green and blue,
They play peek-a-boo, just for you.

Gas clouds fluff and twist about,
Puffed up cheeks, there is no doubt.
While twinkling stars, they blink and play,
Creating constellations in their way.

A cosmic tickle, stars unite,
Floating fuzz in the curtain of night.
They scatter laughter, loud and free,
Painting joy across the galaxy.

So let's embrace this dreamy space,
Where silliness finds its place.
Amongst the glow, the fun ignites,
In the soft embrace of stellar nights.

Cosmic Caper Chronicles

In the dark of night, stars play hide and seek,
Planets spin in twirls, giggling with a squeak.
Asteroids throw parties, oh what a sight,
Comets race by, full of glee and delight.

Aliens in costumes, dancing on the moon,
Wobbling like jelly, to a jazzy tune.
Nebulas in colors, like candy canes bright,
Whispering secrets, under starlight so light.

Saturn's rings jingle, like bells in the sky,
While Pluto grumbles softly, "Why can't I fly?"
Galaxies gather, to share in the fun,
Making a ruckus, until rise of the sun.

What a cosmic circus, this universe wide,
With laughter and joy, there's no need to hide.
Every twinkle and shimmer, a part of the game,
In this galactic playground, joy's never the same.

Starry Shenanigans

Shooting stars giggle, racing through the night,
Sprinkling sparkles, causing pure delight.
Dancing meteors twirl, in a wild, silly trance,
While moonbeams ignite a whimsical dance.

Planets in pajamas, chuckle with the sun,
Twirling around, it's great cosmic fun.
Jupiter tells jokes, with his deep, booming voice,
While Venus just pouts, "Hey, I had no choice!"

Black holes make faces, sucking up the cheer,
With laughter echoing, it's so crystal clear.
Galactic goofballs, shooting across the sky,
Creating a universe where silliness can fly.

Meteor showers fall, like sprinkles made of light,
Every laugh a sparkle, in the cool of the night.
Cosmic capers abound, in this starry parade,
With joy and jest shining brightly, never to fade.

Cosmic Capers

In a dance of stardust, comets start to twirl,
Silly space critters, giving the cosmos a whirl.
Planets stick out tongues, in a cheeky jest,
Wobbling and giggling, having the best quest.

Aliens on bicycles, zooming through the void,
With little green hats, they can't be annoyed.
Each star winks and chuckles, teasing the next,
As constellations plot their whimsical text.

Suns have sunburns, they're feeling quite hot,
While Saturn's rings shimmer, in a dreamy spot.
Galaxies snicker, as they twist and bend,
Creating a tapestry, where humor won't end.

Every tick of the clock, in this vast, silly space,
Marks laughter and joy, on a grand, cosmic race.
In the playground of stars, with bubbles of glee,
The universe spins on, full of whimsy and spree.

Lunar Laughter

On the moon, there's a party, with astronauts in hats,
Playing hide and seek with some silly, space bats.
Rockets are giggling, zooming to the beat,
While craters are singing, oh what a treat!

Stars are throwing confetti, in a dazzling display,
As meteors tumble joyfully, all over the way.
The Milky Way sparkles, in laughter and joy,
While cosmic balloons float, from planet to boy.

Pluto-cheeked with laughter, he dances around,
While the sun claps its rays, sharing cheer all around.
Nebulas twirl like ribbons, in a colorful spree,
As space critters frolic, so wild and so free.

What joy there is, in this vast cosmic show,
With giggles and grins, there's plenty to sow.
Each moment a treasure, in this playful embrace,
Where laughter echoes endlessly, in infinite space.

Twinkling Tickle Fights

Stars giggle in the dark,
They chase comets with a spark.
Moonbeams tease in cosmic ballet,
While planets spin and join the play.

A solar breeze whispers a joke,
As stardust tickles, giggles woke.
The Milky Way joins in the jest,
Creating laughter that feels like rest.

Neptune's rings throw playful darts,
While Venus snickers and outsmarts.
Asteroids roll with a chuckle loud,
In this universe, silly and proud.

With every wink from a distant light,
Even black holes can laugh at night.
In the vastness where dreams ignite,
Twinkling tickle fights take flight!

Comedic Cosmos

In the vastness, humor flows,
Galaxies laugh as a new star glows.
Saturn grins with its goofy rings,
While Uranus jests, and the laughter springs.

Shooting stars slide on banana peels,
Wobbling planets do cartwheels.
Nebulas wear playful hats of mist,
In this cosmic dance, joy can't be missed.

A space whale sings with tone sublime,
Tickling asteroids in a funny rhyme.
Quasars quip with stellar flair,
In this comedic void, we've not a care.

In every twinkle and every grin,
A universe of laughter spins.
Amongst the planets, bright and bold,
The comedic cosmos never gets old.

Flirty Flares

A sunbeam winks from afar,
While flares dance like a shooting star.
Venus blushes in amber glow,
Whispering secrets that only stars know.

Flirty sparks in the Milky haze,
Enchanting the night with a cheeky blaze.
Cosmic giggles sprinkle the void,
In this radiant realm, joy is deployed.

Comets flirt with tails so bright,
As planets tease in the still of night.
Starlit romances in endless flight,
Creating a story of pure delight.

With every angle, a wink appears,
A celestial game that lasts for years.
In this glittering sky, hearts ignite,
Flares of feeling, ever so light.

Dance of the Drifting Asteroids

Asteroids waltz in the dark of space,
Twirling slowly with an elegant grace.
They bump and giggle, crash and spin,
In a rock 'n' roll of laughter and din.

One trips and tumbles with a squeaky sound,
While others spin wildly, twirling around.
Their cosmic dance is a playful sight,
Bouncing through the ether, day and night.

With every twist, they shine and gleam,
In this playful ballet, they live the dream.
Dancing while dodging a comet or two,
Asteroids revel in the joy, it's true!

In the grand scheme, they find delight,
In the simple joys of their silly flight.
So let them drift in their merry spree,
As constellations cheer in harmony.

Merry Meteors

Falling stars do dance and play,
In a sky of silly ballet.
With twirls and flips, they zip about,
Making wishes scream and shout.

They giggle as they blaze on by,
Leaving trails that tickle the sky.
A comet's tail, a wild surprise,
Like candy floss, it waves and flies.

When night arrives, they laugh and swoop,
A cosmic, merry, glowing troop.
With every flash, they spark delight,
In the dark, a twinkling light.

Oh, how they spin, the jolly crew,
Bringing joy with every view.
In the universe's grand parade,
Their laughter echoes, never fade.

Jesting Jupiter

Jupiter jumps with a buoyant bounce,
His storms swirl like a jester's flounce.
With a grin that's larger than the Moon,
  He chuckles to a spaced-out tune.

His moons play tag, they zip and zoom,
In a cosmic game, they twirl and fume.
  A wacky dance on rings of gas,
Each spin and twist is a wiggly pass.

With every swirl, he gives a wink,
  A puffy giant on the brink.
He giggles with a thunderous roar,
His laughter echoes forevermore.

In swirling storms and vibrant hues,
  The jester of the skies imbues.
A rollicking realm of humor divine,
  In Jupiter's grin, the stars align.

Gravitational Guffaws

Gravity pulls with a playful hand,
Making planets do a silly stand.
From wobbling Earth to twirling Mars,
They all join in, the cosmic stars.

A black hole chuckles in the void,
Swallowing light, quite overjoyed.
Spinning like a top in glee,
A vacuum of jokes, can't you see?

Asteroids tumble, with giggly frowns,
In this space of zigzag towns.
The Milky Way laughs with a shine,
Ballet of worlds, in perfect line.

Each galactic giggle, a cosmic cheer,
In a void where silliness appears.
From flinging moons to starry claw,
The universe beams with gravitational guffaws.

Orbiting Oddballs

Around the Sun, they spin and sway,
A troupe of planets in a crazy play.
Each one dons a quirky hat,
Juggling comets as they chat.

Venus winks with a cheeky grin,
While Saturn spins with rings to win.
Mars blushes red with laughter loud,
In the galaxy's zaniest crowd.

Pluto peeks from behind a star,
Saying, "Hey there! I'm still a part!"
His tiny giggles fill the space,
In this oddball, stellar race.

With every orbit, they cheer and loop,
Crafting a silly, cosmic troop.
In the vastness, humor flows free,
Orbiting oddballs in jubilee.

Hubble's Humor

In the sky, a giggle glows,
Planets play in silly clothes.
Stars do waltz, they spin and twirl,
Comets giggle, tails unfurl.

A purple moon, with polka dots,
Toaster-shaped, it happily trots.
Nebulas wear their fluffiest hair,
While asteroids dance without a care.

Galaxy's jokes are whispered well,
In cosmic realms where comets swell.
Laughter floats on cosmic seas,
As stardust plays with solar breeze.

In Hubble's lens, the pranks unfold,
Stories of mischief, bright and bold.

Playfully Pulsating Stars

Pulsing stars have tickle fights,
Shooting laughter through the nights.
Winking planets in a race,
Comedy spills through time and space.

Twinkling lights play peek-a-boo,
Dancing dreams in cosmic hue.
Galaxies wobble, laugh a lot,
In their games, the world is hot.

Their funny pranks bring joy so bright,
Giggling comets burst in flight.
Planets hum their jolly tunes,
Bouncing high like joyous balloons.

Under the brush of a twinkling dome,
Stars remind us, we're not alone.

Zany Zeniths

Atop the heavens, quirks abound,
Whirling worlds on merry ground.
Silly suns wear shades so cool,
While meteors skip to cosmic school.

Zany zeniths, twist and glide,
Celestial clowns in cosmic pride.
Orbits twist like pretzels spun,
In a universe that laughs for fun.

Eclipses share their secret jokes,
While black holes play with dreamy folks.
Asteroids tumble, bump and jest,
In this playground of the blessed.

A cosmic chuckle fills the air,
As laughter dances everywhere.

Antics of the Aurora

A curtain of colors winks and sways,
Auroras laugh in whimsical ways.
They doodle dreams with pastel hues,
Painting skies with giggling views.

Electrifying dances blaze through night,
In swirling skirts of sheer delight.
Stars poke fun with shining beams,
While the moon joins in jolly schemes.

Sparkling threads of joy and cheer,
Whispering tales only they hear.
Galactic jesters jump and play,
Crafting smiles in a vibrant display.

In antics bright, they weave the lights,
Bringing joy to the starry sights.

Perky Planetoids

In the playroom of the stars, they spin,
Chasing comets with big grins.
Jupiter juggles asteroids in tow,
While Mercury puts on a dazzling show.

Saturn's rings sing a silly tune,
Dancing with moonbeams, oh what a boon!
Pluto pokes fun, just trying to fit,
In a cosmic game of hide and split.

Mars makes faces, stains from red clay,
Whirling around like it's a ballet.
Neptune giggles with its ocean of dreams,
While space itself bursts at the seams.

These charming sprites float in delight,
Playing all day and into the night.
In their whimsical realm of twinkling spree,
Planetary jesters, pure jubilee.

Laughing Lightyears

A photon's joke travels lightyears far,
Tickling the tail of each distant star.
Quasars chuckle, bursting with mirth,
As they plunge through the giggling earth.

Wormholes wink with a spectral glow,
Offering rides, saying 'Come on, let's go!'
Galactic gaffes echo through space,
Creating uproarious tales to embrace.

In the cosmos, each star is a friend,
Sharing humor that never can end.
Nebulae puff with breathy delight,
As they whisper punchlines into the night.

Across the void where laughter's the law,
Wacky waves without a flaw.
Traveling smoothly on whimsy's beam,
Eternal jesters in a cosmic dream.

Celestial Comedians

Stars in suits, comedic elite,
Crack jokes on cosmic canvases neat.
Comets slide in with rubbery noses,
While asteroids toss out playful poses.

The Milky Way teems with slapstick glee,
Whirling with humor as bright as can be.
Constellations wink, they know the fun,
Telling tales of how they came to run.

A black hole waits for the punchline's cue,
Sucking in laughs, not a moment too few.
Planets giggle in a synchronous spin,
Every orbit's a joke, where the fun begins.

In this space of jesters unbound,
The universe chuckles, resoundingly found.
Through the expanse, where kindness rules,
Even the sun stops to enjoy the fools.

Cosmic Jamboree

Gather round for a celestial spree,
Where the stars put on a jamboree.
Asteroids parade in a glittering line,
Bopping to rhythms of gourmet divine.

The sun leads with a fiery twist,
Winking at planets that can't resist.
A stellar band plays tunes of delight,
While siblings in orbit dance through the night.

Cosmic confetti sprinkles the void,
With every twinkle, laughter deployed.
A waltz of satellites, spinning with cheer,
Underneath the black sky, oh so dear.

Germs of giggles fill the entire space,
Creating a tapestry of good-natured grace.
In this adventure, silly and grand,
Joy in the universe, forever will stand.

A Clown's Guide to the Cosmos

In the sky, balloons float high,
Stars juggle dreams as they pass by.
Planets wear hats and dance around,
While comets throw pies on the ground.

Galaxies giggle as they twirl,
Cosmic clowns give space a whirl.
With spacetime balloons, they soar and dive,
Making wishes come alive!

Asteroids roll like rubber balls,
Playful echoes fill the halls.
With every burst of sparkling light,
They paint the dark with colors bright.

So join the fun, don't be shy,
The universe laughs, give it a try!
With every wink from up above,
Feel the joy and spread the love.

Whirling Winks from the Universe

Stars blink like winks at night,
Planets spin in pure delight.
Meteors dash in silly lines,
Galactic giggles fill the pines.

Nebulas swirl in cotton candy,
While comets laugh, a bit less dandy.
Moonbeams bounce on laughter's wings,
Creating joy, oh what fun it brings!

Black holes play hide and seek,
Swallowing light, yet still so cheek!
Saturn grins with rings so bright,
Making every asteroid dance in flight.

So spin and twirl with glee,
Join the cosmic jubilee!
In this party of radiant hues,
Find your smile amidst the views.

Celestial Circus

Under the vast starlit dome,
Circus stars feel right at home.
Big top made of swirling mist,
Where even the planets can't resist!

Juggling moons in a playful show,
With giggling suns that steal the glow.
Martians leap, and Venus claps,
While laughter echoes in cosmic laps.

Galactic bears on unicycles ride,
With cosmic acrobats flipping wide.
Neptune plays the organ, sweet and bright,
While everyone dances under starlight.

Join the fun, come take a seat,
Where the universe and humor meet.
With every laugh, you'll lift your soul,
In this celestial, silly stroll!

Jovial Journey Through the Milky Way

A merry boat sails through the night,
With stardust snacks, what a delight!
Floating past with giggles galore,
Each star a friend to learn and explore.

Planets wave in hula skirts,
While meteors salsa, do flips and flirts.
The Moon serves cookies, oh so sweet,
In this jovial dance, feel the beat!

Wormholes twist from here to there,
Whisking us off without a care.
Laughing at time like it's a game,
In this cosmic adventure, we're never the same.

So grab a seat, let's sail away,
Through laughter and joy, come what may!
For in this journey where giggles stay,
We find delight in the Milky Way.

www.ingramcontent.com/pod-product-compliance
Lightning Source LLC
Chambersburg PA
CBHW051628160426
43209CB00004B/560